Y0-BVO-705

Chris Leftley

# BEST OF THE WEB
# GEOGRAPHY

G
70
.L44
2004
West

K · G · Saur  München 2004

**Bibliographic information published by Die Deutsche Bibliothek**
Die Deutsche Bibliothek lists this publication in
the Deutsche Nationalbibliografie; detailed bibliographic data
is available in the internet at http://dnb.ddb.de.

⊗

Printed on acid-free paper

© 2004 K. G. Saur Verlag GmbH, München

Printed in Germany
All Rights Strictly Reserved.
No part of this publication may be reproduced, stored in a retrieval system,
or transmitted in any form or by any means, electronic, mechanical,
photocopying, recording, or otherwise,
without permission in writing from the publisher.
Typesetting by Dr. Rainer Ostermann, München.

Printed and Bound by Strauss Offsetdruck, Mörlenbach.

ISBN 3-598-11537-7

# Table of Contents

# About the Author

Chris Leftley has been a professionally Chartered Librarian for over twenty years working for, among others, the Royal Geographical Society, University College London, British Petroleum, University of the South Pacific, and is currently at the University of Oxford. A special interest in Reference work has been much enlivened by the almost overnight arrival of the Internet, and a desire to sort and share this enthusiasm has resulted in this book and series.

Chris is married with children, passionate about rugby, and lives in Oxfordshire.

# Series Preface

The Internet is now irrevocably part of the information culture, and for many is the first port of call when looking for information on a new or unfamiliar subject. Its most usual manifestation is the World Wide Web (usually just *Web*, or *WWW*), and that is principally what we shall deal with here. It is often compared to a huge Library where the books are in random order and there is no catalogue.

The aim of this series is to provide the reader with a key to ordering this chaos: a selected list of quality reviewed sites in the chosen subject area. Having perused the book briefly beforehand, its purpose is to remove the time which can be wasted by sitting down at a search engine screen and saying "Well, what do I do now?", then typing in a single term and getting huge quantities of irrelevant hits.

The sites listed have been chosen for their relevance, accuracy and consistency – they should all still be there by the time you look at them. About 100 sites have been chosen per volume, to save you time and get you to the heart of the matter: whether you are doing a paper on Oceanography, Operas or Ostriches, you should be able to go straight to the key sites and start finding relevant information.

# Preface

*Best of the Web: Geography* is the first volume in the series, and is aimed at both the intending and practising geography student at all levels. It should also assist academics and laymen who wish to brush up their knowledge and see what the Web has to offer.

The basic structure is an introduction to the subject, followed by a subject outline, where the main subject areas are subdivided into more manageable units, and the major sites for those units are listed alphabetically.

Many of these resources could be listed under more than one heading, so the most likely heading has been selected for its place in the listings.

Several entries are representative, for example in the organisations section; many countries have established societies for geography which cover a wide range of resources and activities, and some typical ones are listed to give a flavour of what is available.

The majority of sites listed are free, but where a subscription is required, this is noted – check with your school/ college/ university/ public library.

Site and URL indexes are provided to give as many options as possible to help you locate the best information quickly and effectively.

We provide a contact email address botwg@yahoo.co.uk. Here you can email us about corrections, amendments and so on, which we should be able to incorporate into future editions, which may or may not be entirely digital – watch this space and this website (http://www.saur.de).

# Acknowledgements

The idea for this series came while I was working as Information Services Librarian at the University of the South Pacific Library in Fiji, and I should like to thank Dr Esther Williams, University Librarian, for having had the courage to take me on!

Gerrie Turpie at K. G. Saur has been a constant encouragement, with lots of excellent ideas, and Claudia Heyer edited assiduously.

Finally, my wife Becky, and the boys, Ben and Tom, without whom …

# Introduction

## What is Geography?

Geography is a very broad church, and has always eluded a completely satisfactory definition of all its areas of study. Perhaps a quotation[1] from the Royal Geographical Society (entry no. 46), founded in 1830 and the oldest geography-oriented body in the English-speaking world, will help set the framework:

"Geography is the integrated study of the earth's landscapes, peoples, places and environments. It is, quite simply, about the world in which we live. It is unique in bridging the social sciences (Human Geography) with its understanding of the dynamics of cultures, societies and economies, and the earth sciences (Physical Geography) in the understanding of the dynamics of physical landscapes and environmental processes. Geography puts this understanding of social and physical processes within the essential context of places and regions – recognising the great differences in cultures, political systems, economies, landscapes and environments across the world, and the links between them. Understanding the causes of differences and inequalities between places and social groups underlie much of the newer developments in Human Geography.

While each of the two broad areas of Human and Physical Geography exists in its own right, the subject also combines them to provide a much-needed capability to study and understand interactions between people, and between people and the physical environments in which they live and upon which they ultimately depend, both locally and globally. This is the core of Geography. In its role as an integrating discipline, Geography provides an ideal framework for relating other fields of knowledge. It is not surprising that those trained as geographers often contribute substantially to the applied management of resources and environments."[1]

---

[1] By kind permission of the Royal Geographical Society.

# Geography on the Web

# Geography on the Web – General resources

## Libraries and their catalogues

Entry number     1
Title     *LibWeb*
URL     http://sunsite.berkeley.edu/Libweb/

Review
*LibWeb* is a listing of major libraries divided by continent, then by country. There is a keyword search option. If available, you can link to the catalogues from the various home pages – useful for tracking down very country-specific data.

| | |
|---|---|
| Owner/Maintainer | UCLA Berkeley |
| Server location | UCLA Berkeley, CA, USA, + eleven mirror sites |
| Authority | * * * * * Comprehensive |
| Ease of use | Click on continent, then country |
| Contact details given | Yes, including author details |
| Links | Good |
| Last update pre-visit | n.d. |
| Alternative languages | No |
| Audience | Academic. General |
| Keywords | Libraries, Catalogues, OPACs |

Entry number     2
Title     *National Libraries of Europe*
URL     http://www.bl.uk/gabriel/index. html

Review
*Gabriel* is the World Wide Web server for Europe's National Libraries. The site operates on four levels, the last of which is where links are offered to pages in which online services of the chosen library are described, e.g. WWW and gopher services;

*General resources*

FTP servers; OPACs; national union catalogues; national bibliographies; special databases, etc. Information on how to log in (if appropriate) is incorporated. On the welcome page select The National Libraries of Europe to get a country listing (41 links), and go the country of your choice. Good for hard to find / nation-specific data (in the original language!).

| | |
|---|---|
| Owner/Maintainer | Gabriel |
| Server location | Choice of five mirrored |
| Authority | * * * * * |
| Ease of use | Good |
| Contact details given | Yes |
| Links | Plenty |
| Last update pre-visit | n.d. |
| Alternative languages | French, German, plus language of national library |
| Audience | Academic, students, teachers, researchers |
| Keywords | Europe, Libraries, Catalogues, OPACs |


| | |
|---|---|
| Entry number | 3 |
| Title | *COPAC* |
| URL | http://www.copac.ac.uk/ |

Review

COPAC is a combined catalogue of 25 of the major academic and research institutions in the UK. The simple form enables you to search several million items simultaneously, and results may be displayed in a variety of ways. Excellent bibliographic tool.

| | |
|---|---|
| Owner/Maintainer | Victoria University of Manchester |
| Server location | Manchester |
| Authority | * * * * * Union catalogue of 25 UK major academic libraries |
| Ease of use | Simple form |
| Contact details given | Yes |
| Links | Internal |
| Last update pre-visit | n.d. |

Alternative languages  No
Audience               General
Keywords               Libraries, Catalogues


Entry number           4
Title                  *OBI – OPACs in Britain and Ireland
                       (NISS)*
URL                    http://www.hero.ac.uk./niss/
                       niss_library4008.cfm

Review

This directory contains details of networked British and Irish library catalogue services (OPACs) in the education, research and public sectors, and includes postal and electronic mail addresses, telephone and fax numbers. Most entries contain direct links to the library's OPAC and to the library's web page, so you can access bibliographic details. You can also search by subject. Comprehensive.

Owner/Maintainer       Annette Lafford, National Information
                       Services and Systems
Server location        n.d.
Authority              * * * * *
Ease of use            Very clear
Contact details given  Yes
Links                  Mainly internal
Last update pre-visit  n.d.
Alternative languages  No
Audience               Academic, students, researchers,
                       teachers
Keywords               Libraries, Catalogues, OPACs

Entry number       5
Title              *British Library*
URL                http://blpc.bl.uk/

Review

The British Library has been collecting materials for around 250 years, and is also a copyright deposit Library, so is one of the ultimate bibliographic resources. Click the SEARCH option to get a clear form to fill in your search query – help is given. Don't forget to click the All Material option to ensure that the search is comprehensive. Excellent bibliographic tool.

Owner/Maintainer       British Library
Server location        British Library, London
Authority              * * * * * Catalogue of the largest Library in the UK
Ease of use            Simple form
Contact details given  Yes
Links                  Internal
Last update pre-visit  n.d.
Alternative languages  No
Audience               General
Keywords               Library, Catalogues, OPACs

# Bibliographies and indexes

Entry number       6
Title              *Geobase*
URL                http://arc.uk.ovid.com/

Review

*Geobase* is an index of bibliographic information in human g., physical g., ecology, geology, oceanography, earth sciences, marine science and development going back to 1994. It is the equivalent of *Geographical Abstracts: Physical* and *Human Geography; Ecological Abstracts*, and others. It currently covers over 1,700 journals, with archive records for many thousand more. Over 70,000 records are added annually, and 99.5% of them have abstracts. Books, conference proceedings, maps, theses etc. are also included. Good for multidisciplinary searches. Accessible in several ways, but basically a subscription based service, so see your Library for access details. Also available as a set of CD-ROMs, updated quarterly.

| | |
|---|---|
| Owner/Maintainer | Elsevier/SilverPlatter/Geo Abstracts |
| Server location | London |
| Authority | * * * * * |
| Ease of use | Simple search once you have got in |
| Contact details given | Yes |
| Links | good |
| Last update pre-visit | n.d. |
| Alternative languages | Depends of language of original |
| Audience | General. Scientific. Academic. |
| Keywords | [All], Indexes |

| | |
|---|---|
| Entry number | 7 |
| Title | *Web of Science* |
| URL | http://wos.mimas.ac.uk/ |

Review

The Web of Science contains the online version of Social Sciences and Science Citation Indexes, which hold millions of references in indexes and contents pages of journals. You can search by author or keyword bring up references to / abstracts of articles.

| | |
|---|---|
| Owner/Maintainer | MIMAS |
| Server location | Manchester, UK |
| Authority | * * * * |
| Ease of use | Good – but subscription only, check with your Library |
| Contact details given | Yes |
| Links | internal |
| Last update pre-visit | 24 days |
| Alternative languages | No |
| Audience | Academic |
| Keywords | [All], Indexes |

| | |
|---|---|
| Entry number | 8 |
| Title | *American Geographical Society Collection* |
| URL | http://leardo.lib.uwm.edu/intro.html |

Review

The scope of the collection is broad, encompassing all aspects of geography, cartography and selected facets of related disciplines such as history, anthropology, archaeology, sociology, demography, economics, geology, oceanography, meteorology, urban studies, travel, discovery and exploration, and materials on human beings as builders and despoilers of the environment. Click on the links to Current Geographical Publications [entry 33] and Online Geographical Bibliography to search the database and retrieve bibliographic information.

| | |
|---|---|
| Owner/Maintainer | American Geographical Society |
| Server location | U. Wisconsin-Milwaukee, Milwaukee, WI, USA |
| Authority | * * * * *one of the world's largest societies and collections |
| Ease of use | * * * * * |
| Contact details given | Yes |
| Links | Good |
| Last update pre-visit | 13 |
| Alternative languages | No |
| Audience | General. Academic |
| Keywords | Area Studies, Statistics, Indexes |

# Subject gateways

| | |
|---|---|
| Entry number | 9 |
| Title | *About Geography* |
| URL | http://geography.about.com/mbody.htm |

Review

A very chatty sponsored site, with current news on the home page, and a frame listing further resources including Cartography/Maps, Census/ Population, Cities & Transport, Climate

& Weather, Country Facts, Cultural Geography, Disasters/ Hazards, GIS & GPS, Latitude/Longitude, Maps, Physical Geography, Rivers and Streams, Time & Time Zones, World Population. America-focussed.

| | |
|---|---|
| Owner/Maintainer | Matt Rosenberg |
| Server location | USA |
| Authority | * * * |
| Ease of use | Good |
| Contact details given | Yes |
| Links | Internal and External |
| Last update pre-visit | 1 |
| Alternative languages | No |
| Audience | General |
| Keywords | [All] Cartography, Population, Urban studies, Transport, Meteorology, Area studies, Latitude/Longitude, GIS, River, Time |

| | |
|---|---|
| Entry number | 10 |
| Title | *Argus Clearinghouse* |
| URL | http://www.clearinghouse.net/ searchbrowse.html |

Review

Argus Clearinghouse was one of the first attempts to categorise and annotate web resources. Although it has recently announced it will no longer be maintained, data will transferred to the Internet Public Library (http://www.ipl.org/). Selecting Earth Sciences gives choices including cartography, climate research, edaphology, geography, geology, geomorphology, geophysics, geosciences, GIS, hydrology, mapping, marine geology, meteorology, natural resources, oceanography, pedology, soil science, water, weather. Other selections available are Area Studies, Environment, Places & People. Each link is annotated.

| | |
|---|---|
| Owner/Maintainer | Argus Associates |
| Server location | USA |
| Authority | * * * * * |
| Ease of use | Good |

*General resources*

| | |
|---|---|
| Contact details given | Yes |
| Links | Annotated |
| Last update pre-visit | 209 |
| Alternative languages | No |
| Audience | General. Academic |
| Keywords | Area studies, cartography, edaphology, environment, geology, geomorphology, geophysics, GIS, hydrology, maps, marine geology, meteorology, oceanography, pedology, water. |

| | |
|---|---|
| Entry number | 11 |
| Title | *BUBL* |
| URL | http://bubl.ac.uk/ |

Review

A national information source for the higher education community, comprising 12,000 selected and catalogued internet resources in all subjects. Click on BUBL links, select G from the alphabetical list and you will get Geographical data, Geography education, Geography links, Geography research, Geography societies. Selecting, Geography links gives 12 resources, each of which is annotated. Then click further, e.g. *SOSIG World Catalogue: Social Geography* gives a list of 74 links titles, e.g. Psychogeography. Indispensable.

| | |
|---|---|
| Owner/Maintainer | U. of Strathclyde, Glasgow |
| Server location | Glasgow, UK |
| Authority | * * * * * Oldest and most enduring |
| Ease of use | * * * * * |
| Contact details given | Yes |
| Links | * * * * *hierarchical, well organised |
| Last update pre-visit | n.d. |
| Alternative languages | No |
| Audience | Anyone interested in any (academic) subject |
| Keywords | [Type in anything at http://bubl.ac.uk/link/] |

| Entry number | 12 |
|---|---|
| Title | *GeoExplorer* |
| URL | http://www.geoexplorer.co.uk/ |

With kind permission of GeoExplorer – The Geography Portal.

Review

A site full of links and resources to support students and teachers of geography and those with a general interest in geography – Free outline maps of the countries/continents of the world; GeoFacts – A selection of interesting / fascinating facts on geography grouped alphabetically; GeoExplorer Dictionary and Geography Glossaries; A collection of photos from around the world; A selection of cartoons with a geographical theme; GeoNewsNetwork – up-to-date news feeds from over a thousand newspapers and journals worldwide; Guide to Remote Sensing, including an archive of satellite images listed by theme, includes images of countries/ regions as well as images of key geographical features and processes. Screen Saver – to brighten up the desktop and give it a geographical theme.

*General resources*

From the homepage, click on WebLinkBank to access over 2,500 annotated and ranked online resources. Cheerful and unpretentious. Part of the Geography Web Ring [entry 15].

| | |
|---|---|
| Owner/Maintainer | G Richards |
| Server location | UK |
| Authority | * * * * * |
| Ease of use | Simple |
| Contact details given | Yes |
| Links | Internal |
| Last update pre-visit | 1 |
| Alternative languages | No |
| Audience | General. Academic |
| Keywords | News, Remote Sensing, Maps |

| | |
|---|---|
| Entry number | 13 |
| Title | *Geography Arena* |
| URL | http://www.geographyarena.com/geographyarena/home/home.htm |

Review

This is an example of a commercial site offering its range of materials – here, the Geography subset, for general browsing e.g. to see tables of contents, with subscriptions where required, e.g. full-text. Clicking on the Journal Resources tab, then Journal details, brings up Development Studies, Environment, Geography, Planning and Transport. There is also an Online Journals link to allow multiple cross-searching to find bibliographic information and abstracts.

| | |
|---|---|
| Owner/Maintainer | Taylor and Francis |
| Server location | UK |
| Authority | * * * * |
| Ease of use | Good |
| Contact details given | Yes |
| Links | Internal |
| Last update pre-visit | 1 |
| Alternative languages | No |

| | |
|---|---|
| Audience | Academic |
| Keywords | Journals |

| | |
|---|---|
| Entry number | 14 |
| Title | *Geography Site* |
| URL | http://www.geography-site.co.uk |

Review

Formerly Geography Exchange, and approved by the National Grid for Learning (NGfL) in the UK. Over 750 links in 30 categories (including Agriculture, Energy, Facts and Figures, GPS, Journals, Maps, Oceanography, Population, Remote Sensing, Hydrology and Meteorology) make this an excellent starting-point. Also part of the Geography Web-Ring [entry 15] (which brings together geography-oriented sites across the internet and thus provides a central resource for anyone interested in Geography).

| | |
|---|---|
| Owner/Maintainer | David Robinson |
| Server location | UK |
| Authority | * * * * |
| Ease of use | Very good – graphically simple |
| Contact details given | Yes |
| Links | At least 750 external |
| Last update pre-visit | 16 days |
| Alternative languages | No |
| Audience | Academic. General |
| Keywords | Earthquakes, Volcanoes, Plate Tectonics, Structure of the Earth, Glaciers, Rivers, Environment, Agriculture, Energy, Statistics, Journals, Cartography, Oceanography, Population, Remote Sensing, Hydrology, Meteorology |

Entry number       15
Title              *Geography Web Ring*
URL                http://www.zephryus.demon.co.
                   uk/education/webring/

Review
The Geography Web Ring brings together geography sites across the Internet to provide a central resource for anyone interested in Geography. All member sites must provide a free, useful source of information that is acceptable in content and presentation for use by schools, teachers and students. Sites which do not match these criteria will not be admitted to the ring. Each site has links allowing visitors to move from one relevant site to another, without using a search engine. Sites are linked so that they form a virtual ring; if you visit all the sites you'll eventually end up where you started. There are currently 99 sites.

Owner/Maintainer        n.d.
Server location         UK
Authority               * * * *
Ease of use             Good
Contact details given   Only general Ring support
Links                   Internal
Last update pre-visit   1
Alternative languages   No
Audience                General. Academic
Keywords                Human g., Physical g, Environment,
                        Maps, Population, Reference,
                        Organisations

| Entry number | 16 |
| --- | --- |
| Title | *Geography World* |
| URL | http://www.members.aol.com/ bowermanb/101.html |

Review

This site is aimed primarily at Geography 101 students in the USA, and has a colourful visual index on the home page, consisting of large buttons, e.g. Latin America Culture/Geography, Earthquakes/Volcanoes. Each of these is well-linked, and a quiz is usually provided.

Existing services are used in the links, e.g. geography.about. com [entry 9], but the style and breadth of this site makes it useful, particularly for the non-specialist.

Part of the Geography Webring [entry 15], which brings together Geography sites on the Internet for schools, students and teachers.

| Owner/Maintainer | Brad Bowerman |
| --- | --- |
| Server location | Pennsylvania, USA |
| Authority | * * * One man site, but a labour of love |
| Ease of use | Click and go |
| Contact details given | Yes |
| Links | * * * * * plenty, but some breaks |
| Last update pre-visit | n.d. |
| Alternative languages | No |
| Audience | General |
| Keywords | Culture, Earthquakes, Volcanoes |

| Entry number | 17 |
| --- | --- |
| Title | *Geo-Guide* |
| URL | http://www.geo-guide.de |

Review

On the home page, there are three main options, of which the Subject Catalogue, although geared towards earth sciences, is most useful. Hierarchically ordered, selecting Geography brings up a choice of four sub-divisions: physical, human, applied and regional. Clicking on Human brings up eight links, available at a glance and star rated for contents, clarity, index and links. Choosing Population Geography brings up eight links. Choosing Population pyramids opens up another browser window, and selecting from a range of options offered by the US Census Bureau, International Database [entry 85], you can quickly construct a pyramid for the country of your choice. The Subject Catalogue lists, in addition to Geography, Earth Sciences, Geology, Mineralogy, Geochemistry, Petrology, Mineral Deposits, Geophysics, Geodesy, Meteorology and Climatology, Hydrology, Oceanography, Soil Science, GIS, Cartography and Maps. The other two options on the home page are a Source Type (including Journals, Software, Bibliography), and a Search Engine option. You can also view the most recently added records to the database, in alphabetical sequence.

| | |
|---|---|
| Owner/Maintainer | State and University Library, Göttingen, Germany |
| Server location | State and University Library, Göttingen, Germany |
| Authority | Highly respected Libraries |
| Ease-of-use | Clear and well thought out |
| Contact details given | Yes |
| Links | All selected and evaluated |
| Last update pre-visit | 37 days |
| Alternative languages | None |
| Audience | General. Academic |
| Keywords | Human geography, Physical geography, Cartography, Maps, Earth Sciences, Geology, Mineralogy, Geochemistry, Petrology, Mineral deposits, Geophysics, Geodesy, Meteorology and Climatology, Hydrology, Oceanography, Soil Science, GIS. |

| Entry number | 18 |
|---|---|
| Title | *Geosource* |
| URL | http://www.library.uu.nl/geosource/ |

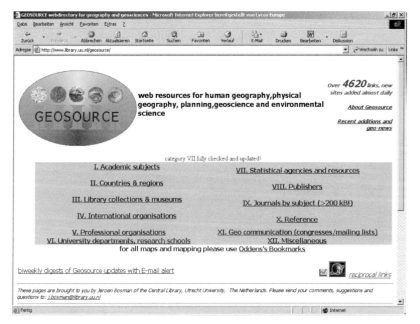

With kind permission of J. Bosman, Utrecht University Library.

Review

*Geosource* aims to provide an extensive and thoroughly categorised subject gateway to relevant web pages. The Home page
includes the following major sub-divisions: Academic resources
(which leads to Resources by discipline/subject, with 13 headings containing 164 links), Statistical agencies and resources,
Countries & regions, Library collections & museums, Journals
by subject, International / Professional organisations, Reference, University departments and research schools. You can
sign up for a biweekly email alert.

| | |
|---|---|
| Owner/Maintainer | Jeroen Bosman |
| Server location | Utrecht University, Netherlands |
| Authority | * * * * |
| Ease of use | Very good – well designed |
| Contact details given | Yes |

*General resources*

| | |
|---|---|
| Links | Good |
| Last update pre-visit | Updated almost daily |
| Alternative languages | No (depends on language of original) |
| Audience | Academic |
| Keywords | [All] Cartography, Environmental Science and Policy Studies, Human Geography, Physical Geography, Planning Science |

| | |
|---|---|
| Entry number | 19 |
| Title | *GESource* |
| URL | http://www.gesource.ac.uk/home.html |

Review

GESource is the geography and environment hub of the Resource Discovery Network (*RDN*). It provides access to high quality Internet resources for students, researchers and practitioners in geography and the environment through five distinct subject gateways: *Environment, General Geography, Human Geography, Physical Geography*, and *Techniques and Approaches*. Each of these main headings is further divided into a series of sub-sections that together make up the browse structure of GESource.

Each resource in the main GESource catalogue has been selected by information professionals and subject specialists to ensure relevance and quality. A full description of each resource is provided, together with a range of other information and direct access to the resource itself. Due to the interdisciplinary nature of geographical and environmental studies, GESource includes in its catalogue resources originating from other hubs within the RDN providing a single access point to this information: look at the list of Databases. Indispensable

| | |
|---|---|
| Owner/Maintainer | *CALIM* (Consortium of Academic Libraries in Manchester) |
| Server location | Manchester, UK |
| Authority | * * * * * |

| | |
|---|---|
| Ease of use | Type and go |
| Contact details given | Yes |
| Links | Plentiful |
| Last update pre-visit | 1 |
| Alternative language | No |
| Audience | Academic. General |
| Keywords | [All] |

| | |
|---|---|
| Entry number | 20 |
| Title | *HUMBUL (Humanities Bulletin Board)* |
| URL | http://www.humbul.ac.uk |

Review

This is the Humanities Hub for the Resource Discovery Network (RDN) located in Oxford. Although Geography is not listed as a subject on the Homepage, entering it as a keyword at the Search HUMBUL button brings up several links, and the site offers geography-related resources.

| | |
|---|---|
| Owner/Maintainer | HUMBUL, University of Oxford |
| Server location | University of Oxford, UK |
| Authority | * * * * * indispensable |
| Ease of use | Good |
| Contact details given | Yes |
| Links | high quality |
| Last update pre-visit | 90 days |
| Alternative languages | No |
| Audience | Academic |
| Keywords | [All] |

*General resources*

| | |
|---|---|
| Entry number | 21 |
| Title | *INFOMINE* |
| URL | http://infomine.ucr.edu/ |

Review

INFOMINE is a unique Web resource featuring well organised access to important university level research and educational tools on the Internet. A virtual library, INFOMINE is notable for its collection of annotated and indexed links. Information in INFOMINE is easy to find given the multiplicity of access points provided (ways of finding the information contained). Twelve databases are listed on the homepage, most of which are relevant to the geographer. A search on Geography brings up over 400 hits with brief comments on each resource, but they are not categorised. Good quality links.

| | |
|---|---|
| Owner/Maintainer | Wendie Helms |
| Server location | U. California, Riverside, USA |
| Authority | * * * * * |
| Ease of use | Well organised |
| Contact details given | Yes |
| Links | Internal |
| Last update pre-visit | 7 |
| Alternative languages | No |
| Audience | Academic |
| Keywords | [All] |

| | |
|---|---|
| Entry number | 22 |
| Title | *Internet Geographer* |
| URL | http://www.internetgeographer.co.uk/index.html |

Review

Internet Geographer is a project that aims to give easier access to the vast array of useful resources on the internet. It is a directory of useful web sites. These are grouped in different aspects of Geography. From the contents page or navigation frame, click on the link for the aspect of Geography that you are interested in, read the brief descriptions and star rating.

Click on the hypertext link if it seems worth a visit. There is also a search facility which lets you do a keyword search of the database of links.
Includes World Population Clock, and is a member of the Geography Web Ring [entry 15].

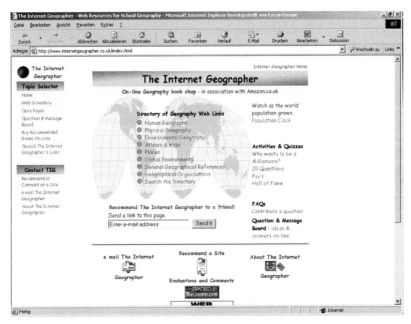

With kind permission of Kevin Hughes, ICT & Geography Education Consultant.

| Owner/Maintainer | Kevin Hughes |
|---|---|
| Server location | UK |
| Authority | * * * * |
| Ease of use | Good |
| Contact details given | Yes |
| Links | Annotated, some broken |
| Last update pre-visit | 1 |
| Alternative languages | No |
| Audience | General. Academic. |
| Keywords | Human g., Physical g, Weather, Atlases & Maps |

*General resources*

| | |
|---|---|
| Entry number | 23A & 23B |
| Title | *Internet Geographer* (RDN Virtual Training Suite) |
| URL | http://www.vts.rdn.ac.uk/tutorial/geographer |
| Title | *Internet Earth Scientist* (RDN Virtual Training Suite) |
| URL | http://www.vts.rdn.ac.uk/tutorial/earth |

Review

The Resource Discovery Network (RDN) is a co-operative academic community run by UKOLN and King's College London. The aim is to provide high quality resources for the learning and research communities, and it has launched a series of Virtual Training Suites by subject. They are well written, always with the student in mind, and include a tour of key sites for the subject, ways of improving your internet searching and thinking about the way the internet can be more effectively used, with reviews and a quiz. They are simple, logical and an excellent introduction to effective internet usage.

| | |
|---|---|
| Owner/Maintainer | SOSIG |
| Server location | UKOLN (U. Bath) and King's College London |
| Authority | * * * * * |
| Ease of use | Well constructed tour |
| Contact details given | Yes, including author details |
| Links | Good and relevant |
| Last update pre-visit | n.d. |
| Alternative languages | No |
| Audience | Academic. General |
| Keywords | Resources, Information Skills |

| | |
|---|---|
| Entry number | 24 |
| Title | *Internet Resources for Geographers* |
| URL | http://www.colorado.edu/ geography/virtdept/resources/ contents.htm |

Review

This page lists the contents of the resources, which are well organised and easy to follow. They include Starting Places, Journals, Professional Associations and Research Organisations, Map collections, Geo-spatial datasets, Newsgroups and Listservs. Also useful miscellaneous sites for Flags of the World, Heads of States (with links to countries), and the Great Globe Gallery [entry 60].

Starting Places is particularly useful, with Search Engines (with tips on use), Resource lists – general and by subject (Cartography, GIS, Remote Sensing, Physical geography), News, References and selected University and Public Libraries.

| | |
|---|---|
| Owner/Maintainer | Anita Howard & Kenneth Forte; Department of Geography, University of Colorado |
| Server location | University of Colorado, Boulder, CO, USA |
| Authority | * * * * * Highly respected Department |
| Ease of use | * * * * * |
| Contact details given | Yes |
| Links | Plenty. Only one or two broken |
| Last update pre-visit | 106 |
| Alternative languages | No |
| Audience | Academic. General |
| Keywords | Journals, Maps, Newsgroups, Flags, GIS, Remote Sensing, Cartography, Libraries, News |

| Entry number | 25 |
|---|---|
| Title | *Nice Geography Sites* |
| URL | http://www.frw.ruu.nl/nicegeo.html |

Review

This quaintly named site is really a list of links, but very comprehensive: General Geography (mainly university geography departments); GIS and Remote Sensing (sites and newsgroups), which are mainly academic, with some commercial, listed alphabetically.

The lists are long, but alphabetisation throws up neighbours like Ordnance Survey (listed as British Ordnance Survey), Fish and Wildlife Service (US), National Snow and Ice Data Center (listed as NSIDC), Palaeomagnetic database for the world and WOCE (World Ocean Circulation Experiment).

| | |
|---|---|
| Owner/Maintainer | M Zeylmans |
| Server location | University of Utrecht, Netherlands |
| Authority | * * * One enthusiast's site |
| Ease of use | Click and go |
| Contact details given | Yes |
| Links | * * * * * Comprehensive |
| Last update pre-visit | 20 days |
| Alternative languages | No – but several Dutch links |
| Audience | Academic |
| Keywords | GIS, Remote sensing, Cartography, Oceanography |

| Entry number | 26 |
|---|---|
| Title | *Social Sciences Information Gateway (SOSIG)* |
| URL | http://www.sosig.ac.uk/geography/ |

Review

One of major gateways for social sciences information, offering access to thousands of quality sources chosen by librarians and subject specialists. Has Thesaurus (list of preferred vocabulary) for efficient searching, and a very useful Browse facility, giving a directory-style interface from which you can select the subject of your choice: Geography divides into Economic g., GIS and cartography, Social g., each of which sub-divides into Collections, Databases, Educational materials, Journals, Reference etc. – see especially Resource Guides.

With kind permission of the Social Science Information Gateway (SOSIG), Institute for Learning and Research Technology, University of Bristol.

| | |
|---|---|
| Owner/Maintainer | A service of the Resource Development Network (RDN) |
| Server location | University of Bristol, UK, mirrored at University of Wisconsin, USA |
| Authority | * * * * * indispensable |
| Ease of use | * * * * |
| Contact details given | Yes |
| Links | * * * * * many and varied |
| Last update pre-visit | 52 |
| Alternative languages | No |
| Audience | Academic. General |
| Keywords | Economic geography, GIS, Cartography, Social geography |

*General resources*

| Entry number | 27 |
| --- | --- |
| Title | *UK Government* |
| URL | http://www.ukonline.gov.uk/Home/ Homepage/fs/en |

Review

The UK Government (like many of its counterparts) publishes a wealth of data on the Web, so it is an excellent starting point for "Official Publications" (e.g. *Census, Annual Abstract of Statistics*). A good feature is that when getting a large number of hits a set of suggested filters comes up to refine the search. May take some time to reach what you want.

| | |
| --- | --- |
| Owner/Maintainer | UK Government |
| Server location | London, UK |
| Authority | * * * * * Government data |
| Ease of use | Select your search topic and go |
| Contact details given | Yes |
| Links | Good |
| Last update pre-visit | n.d. |
| Alternative languages | No |
| Audience | General |
| Keywords | [All], Statistics |

| Entry number | 28 |
| --- | --- |
| Title | *World Wide Web Virtual Library: Geography* |
| URL | http://www.icomos.org/ WWW_VL_Geography.html |

Review

Now hosted by ICOMOS, an international non-governmental organisation of professionals dedicated to the conservation of the world's historic monuments and sites. This is a fairly short eclectic list of links divided into three categories: General, Countries, and Educational Institutions. You can scan it fairly quickly to see if there is anything of interest.

| | |
|---|---|
| Owner/Maintainer | Heather McAdam |
| Server location | Paris |
| Authority | * * * * |
| Ease of use | Simple |
| Contact details given | Yes |
| Links | About 50 |
| Last update pre-visit | 23 days |
| Alternative languages | French |
| Audience | General. Academic |
| Keywords | [All] |

# Current awareness services / mailing-lists

| | |
|---|---|
| Entry number | 29 |
| Title | *SOSIG email alerting service* |
| URL | http://www.sosig.ac.uk/help/custom.html |

Review

If you set up a (free) account at this site, you will be able to customise SOSIG to create your own, tailored SOSIG information services. My Account can help you with: current awareness (receive weekly email notification of new Internet sites, conferences and courses which match your own personal interests, find like-minded colleagues who are working in the same fields as you, find conferences and courses which match your interests); career development (publish your CV on the Grapevine section of SOSIG) and publicity of your conferences and courses. Good way to stay up-to-date.

| | |
|---|---|
| Owner/Maintainer | A service of the Resource Discovery Network (RDN), Institute for Learning and Research Technology, University of Bristol |
| Server location | Bristol, UK |
| Authority | * * * * * Top gateway |
| Ease of use | Register and go |
| Contact details given | Yes |

*General resources*

Links                  Good
Last update pre-visit  n.d.
Alternative languages  No
Audience               General
Keywords               Email, Alerts


Entry number           30
Title                  *Scout Report*
URL                    http://scout.cs.wisc.edu/

Review

Although not strictly speaking a subject-specific resource, the Scout Report is one of the oldest and most respected current awareness services from the USA. Each weeks brings a new serendipity of freshly mounted/discovered sites, often with a geographical component. You can search the Archive by Subject. Subscribe to the free weekly mailing to see What's New. Good for broadening the horizons.

Owner/Maintainer       Internet Scout Project Team
Server location        U. Wisconsin-Madison, USA
Authority              * * * * * Original and best
Ease of use            Good
Contact details given  Yes
Links                  Annotated
Last update pre-visit  1
Alternative languages  No
Audience               General
Keywords               [All]

| Entry number | 31 |
|---|---|
| Title | *Directory of Scholarly and Professional E-Conferences* |
| URL | http://www.kovacs.com/directory |

Review

A directory of academic discussion lists. You can enter a Keyword or search the Broad Category "Social sciences", subcategory "Geography". A good way to keep in touch with people and developments in your field.

| Owner/Maintainer | Diane Kovacs |
|---|---|
| Server location | Brunswick, OH, USA |
| Authority | * * * * * |
| Ease of use | Browse or Enter subject in box and click Find List |
| Contact details given | Yes |
| Links | Few |
| Last update pre-visit | n.d. |
| Alternative languages | No |
| Audience | General. Scientific. Academic |
| Keywords | Mailing list, Discussion list |

# Journals

| Entry number | 32 |
|---|---|
| Title | *Area* |
| URL | http://www.ingenta.com/journals/browse/bpl/area |

Review

*Area* was originally established in 1969 as a bulletin for the Institute of British Geographers, but has evolved into a full academic journal, typically containing shorter, topical articles of scholarly interest to geographers, and is now one of the most widely read and discussed journals in British professional geography. *Area* also serves as a medium for the expression of professional opinion on matters of public interest, and aims to encourage free and impartial discussion of ideas, techniques and findings. Book reviews are incorporated into each issue as page extent allows. Many free articles. Searchable. Available on subscription through your institution's library.

| | |
|---|---|
| Owner/Maintainer | RGS/IBG |
| Server location | UK |
| Authority | * * * * |
| Ease of use | Very simple |
| Contact details given | Yes |
| Links | Internal |
| Last update pre-visit | 60 |
| Alternative languages | No |
| Audience | General. Academic |
| Keywords | Journals |

| | |
|---|---|
| Entry number | 33 |
| Title | *Current Geographical Publications* |
| URL | http://leardo.lib.uwm.edu/cgp/index.html |

Review

*Current Geographical Publications,* which commenced in 1938, is issued ten times a year, monthly except July and August. Bibliographical references to books, periodical articles, pamphlets, government documents, maps and atlases in the American Geographical Society Collection of the University of Wisconsin-Milwaukee are included and arranged in accordance with the classification scheme utilised in the AGS Collection Research Catalogue. The four sections in each issue are: Topical, Regional, Maps, and Selected Books and Monographs. Section IV is an alphabetical listing of selected books arranged by author; each entry in this last section is also listed elsewhere under the appropriate topical or regional category. The ten most recent issues are searchable, to enable you to keep up-to-date.

| | |
|---|---|
| Owner/Maintainer | American Geographical Society |
| Server location | U. Wisconsin, Milwaukee, USA |
| Authority | * * * * * |

| | |
|---|---|
| Ease of use | Simple |
| Contact details given | Yes |
| Links | Mainly unbroken |
| Last update pre-visit | n.d. |
| Alternative languages | No |
| Audience | Academic |
| Keywords | Journals, Indexes |

| | |
|---|---|
| Entry number | 34 |
| Title | *CyberGEO* |
| URL | http://www.cybergeo.presse.fr/ |

Review

*CYBERGEO*, the electronic *European Journal of Geography*, is intended to promote faster communication of research and greater direct contact between authors and readers. Created with the aim of encouraging the exchange of ideas, methods and results, it gives European geographers the possibility of writing in their mother tongues. It deals with the entire range of geographical concerns and interests, with no preferences for any particular school or theme. A high scientific standard is ensured by submitting communications to an international committee of readers. By hosting discussion and mailing lists the journal aims to stimulate open debate and intellectual exchange. Access to the published articles is facilitated by a system of headings and keywords.

| | |
|---|---|
| Owner/Maintainer | Denise Pumain |
| Server location | France |
| Authority | * * * * * |
| Ease of use | Click and go |
| Contact details given | Yes |
| Links | Few |
| Last update pre-visit | n.d. |
| Alternative languages | French. Others according to articles published |
| Audience | General. Scientific. Academic |
| Keywords | [All] |

| | |
|---|---|
| Entry number | 35 |
| Title | *Electronic Resources for Geographers* |
| URL | http://www.acu.edu:9090/ ~armstrongl/geography/geog.htm |

Review

An American site put together by an enthusiastic teacher, aimed at K12 students but with plenty of information – see especially Geography Resources and More Geography Resources. Part of the Geography Web Ring [entry 15].

| | |
|---|---|
| Owner/Maintainer | Lewis Armstrong |
| Server location | Abilene, TX, USA |
| Authority | * * * * |
| Ease of use | Good – searchable |
| Contact details given | Yes |
| Links | Extensive |
| Last update pre-visit | 275 |
| Alternative languages | No – but possible through http://babel. altavista.com/ |
| Audience | Academic. General |
| Keywords | [All] |

| | |
|---|---|
| Entry number | 36 |
| Title | *Geographical Journal (GJ)* |
| URL | http://www.blackwell-synergy.com/ rd.asp?code=geoj&goto=journal |

Review

One of the heavyweight journals in the field, *GJ* publishes original research and scholarship in physical and human geography with particular emphasis placed on environment (change, degradation, policy) and development (economics, education, resource management, aid, and poverty). *GJ* publishes research findings undertaken using the widest range of research approaches, publishing papers of depth and substance which are accessible to a wide audience, encouraging papers from all parts of the world, and ensuring rigorous standards of refereeing. It is also renowned for its invaluable book review section: in addition to short reviews, the journal carries longer, comparative reviews of groups of books related to its mission. The fourth issue of each volume focuses on cartography, interpreted in its widest sense: coverage ranges from GIS and remote sensing to modern and computer mapping. Each issue contains an editorial and / or lead article and book review section dedicated to this theme. Currently goes back to 2001, and full-text is available as .pdf files. You can sign up for a free table of contents alert, and further information is available on subscription – check your Library.

| | |
|---|---|
| Owner/Maintainer | Blackwell Publishing for Royal Geographical Society |
| Server location | Oxford |
| Authority | * * * * * |
| Ease of use | Select required article from list |
| Contact details given | Publisher's |
| Links | Internal |
| Last update pre-visit | n.d. |
| Alternative languages | No |
| Audience | Academic |
| Keywords | [All], Environment, development, cartography, GIS |

| | |
|---|---|
| Entry number | 37 |
| Title | *Geography resources: Journals* |
| URL | http://www.rgs.org/category. php?Page=mainpublications |

Review

Click on other Journals – Geography to get a list of e-journals in the field, a mixture of free and subscription-based resources, but usually with searchable indexes.

| | |
|---|---|
| Owner/Maintainer | Royal Geographical Society / Institute of British Geographers |
| Server location | London, UK |
| Authority | * * * * Original sources |
| Ease of use | Simple |

*General resources*

| | |
|---|---|
| Contact details given | Yes |
| Links | Mainly unbroken |
| Last update pre-visit | n.d. |
| Alternative languages | No |
| Audience | Academic |
| Keywords | Journals, Indexes |

| | |
|---|---|
| Entry number | 38 |
| Title | *Ingenta* [formerly *UnCover*] |
| URL | http://www.ingenta.com/ |

Review

Having bought UnCover, and renamed it, ingenta is a global research gateway providing a free online search service of published content from reliable research sources, giving you free access, where available, to the article summaries of over 25,000 publications and the full-text of over 4,500 publications from 150 publishers (mainly of journals). If you subscribe, the figures change to over 11,000,000 and 26,000. You enter a search in the search articles box or, if you know more or less what you're looking for, use the headings in the Subject Area Resources, of which Earth/Environmental Sciences is one. You then have further sub-headings (Ecology, Geology, Geography, Geophysics and geomagnetism, Meteorology and climatology, and Oceanography). Clicking on Ecology brings up some resources headings, followed by a set of links (including Technical reports, Reference, Environmental law, General data and resources, Global warming and climate change, Oceans, Associations and Metasites). You can also personalise your research, by setting up research and table of content alerts, save searches you have made, access independent research news, and set up a list of your favourite publications. Excellent for article searching.

| | |
|---|---|
| Owner/Maintainer | Exeter College for Ingenta |
| Server location | Exeter College, Oxford, UK |
| Authority | * * * * *Major supplier of journal articles |
| Ease of use | Very good – well designed |

| | |
|---|---|
| Contact details given | Yes |
| Links | Good |
| Last update pre-visit | n.d. |
| Alternative languages | No (depends on language of original) |
| Audience | General. Academic |
| Keywords | [All], Journals, Indexes |

| | |
|---|---|
| Entry number | 39 |
| Title | *Planet Diary* |
| URL | http://www.phschool.com/science/planetdiary/index.html |

Review

Although hosted commercially, the deeper you delve, the more fun this site becomes. It presents weekly geological, biological, environmental, meteorological and astronomical news from around the globe, dating back to January 1998. From the home page you can click on Current Phenomena (incl. view Earth from a satellite), Calendar (incl. forthcoming meteor showers, apogees, eclipses and World xyz day), Universal Measurements (nearly 50 converters, time zones, World population clock), Archive, Phenomena Backgrounders and Guide.

| | |
|---|---|
| Owner/Maintainer | Pearson Education |
| Server location | USA |
| Authority | * * * * |
| Ease of use | Simple and fun |
| Contact details given | Only publisher's homepage |
| Links | Not numerous, but they work |
| Last update pre-visit | n.d. |
| Alternative languages | No |
| Audience | General |
| Keywords | Earth, Geology, Biology, Environment, Meteorology, Astronomy, Maps, Time |

| | |
|---|---|
| Entry number | 40 |
| Title | *Scholarly Articles Research Alerting (SARA)* |
| URL | http://www.tandf.co.uk/sara/ |

Review

SARA is a service designed to deliver by email tables of contents for any issue of Carfax, Martin Dunitz, Psychology Press, Routledge, Spon Press or Taylor & Francis journals to anyone who requests the information. Having registered, selecting Alphabetical Listing, then Geography, Planning and Environment to get a list of titles sub-divided by these three headings, plus Development, European Area Studies and Transport, totalling 68 journals.

See also the listings for Built Environment, GIS/Remote Sensing and Social Sciences, which includes Area studies

| | |
|---|---|
| Owner/Maintainer | Taylor and Francis |
| Server location | London |
| Authority | * * * * Commercial |
| Ease of use | Good |
| Contact details given | Yes |
| Links | Good |
| Last update pre-visit | n.d. |
| Alternative languages | No |
| Audience | General |
| Keywords | Planning, Environment, Development, Europe, Transport, Area Studies |

| | |
|---|---|
| Entry number | 41 |
| Title | *Topica Exchange* |
| URL | http://www.topica.com/dir/?cid=0 |

Review

Topica Ltd. provides email newsletter publishers, from multinational media companies to individuals publishing news about a hobby or interest. Topica's flagship service, Topica Exchange, is a free email publishing service serving more than

70,000 individual publishers and delivering 100,000 newsletters. Typing in Geograph* in the Search box brings up around 40 matches, and they are very diverse; a little digging should uncover your special field.

| | |
|---|---|
| Owner/Maintainer | Topica Ltd |
| Server location | n.d. |
| Authority | * * * |
| Ease of use | * * * * * Start from Directory page |
| Contact details given | Yes |
| Links | Internal |
| Last update pre-visit | n.d. |
| Alternative languages | No |
| Audience | General |
| Keywords | Email, Alerts, Discussion |


| | |
|---|---|
| Entry number | 42 |
| Title | *Transactions of the Institute of British Geographers* |
| URL | http://www.rgs.org/templ.php?page=8publetr |

Review

One of the major journals in the field, *TIBG* is an international quarterly journal of geographical research. It publishes substantial, internationally refereed articles of the highest scholarly standard on any theoretical or empirical subject in Geography, and reviews books across the full spectrum of the discipline. Provides free access to the 1500 articles published in the journal since its first issue in 1935 up until 1995. Searchable by author, title, year and key words, articles can be downloaded and read as .pdf files. Post-1996 articles are available to subscribers through Ingenta.com. [entry 38]. Very important journal.

| | |
|---|---|
| Owner/Maintainer | Royal Geographical Society / Institute of British Geographers |
| Server location | London, UK |
| Authority | * * * * * |
| Ease of use | Good – searchable |

*General resources*

| | |
|---|---|
| Contact details given | Yes |
| Links | Internal |
| Last update pre-visit | n.d. |
| Alternative languages | No |
| Audience | Academic |
| Keywords | Journals |

| | |
|---|---|
| Entry number | 43 |
| Title | *Working Papers in Geography* |
| URL | http://www.geog.ox.ac.uk/~jburke/ wpapers/index.html |

Review

The Economic Geography Research Group has produced around over 100 *Working Papers* to date, and all current issues are presented in .pdf format. Copies of past papers are not downloadable: published working papers can be found in their respective journals, unpublished working papers can be obtained from the Department. They are listed chronologically, so there is no subject access. Topics covered include Privatising Water in England and Wales, France's regional Unemployment Problem, The City of London in the Asian Crisis. Very authoritative.

| | |
|---|---|
| Owner/Maintainer | Jan Burke, Dept. of Geography, U. of Oxford |
| Server location | Oxford, UK |
| Authority | * * * * * Top University Department |
| Ease of use | Good – papers indexed chronologically |
| Contact details given | Yes |
| Links | Internal |
| Last update pre-visit | 7 |
| Alternative languages | No |
| Audience | Academic |

# Organisations

| | |
|---|---|
| Entry number | 44 |
| Title | *Association of American Geographers (AAG)* |
| URL | http://www.aag.org/ |

Review

The oldest-established American scientific and educational society for geographers, founded in 1904. This is a well organised and easily navigable site, with all aspects of the AAG's work covered, (including Careers, Education, Grants and awards, Publications, What's new! and What's news). Related organisations is a useful link, and also helps with Canadian and Latin American studies.

| | |
|---|---|
| Owner/Maintainer | Association of American Geographers, USA |
| Server location | Washington, DC, USA |
| Authority | * * * * * |
| Ease of use | * * * * * scrollable frames |
| Contact details given | Yes |
| Links | Mostly internal |
| Last update pre-visit | 75 |
| Alternative languages | No |
| Audience | Academic. General |
| Keywords | Education, Careers, Publications, News |

| | |
|---|---|
| Entry number | 45 |
| Title | *Geographical Association (GA)* |
| URL | http://www.geography.org.uk/ |

Review

Although aimed principally at the school child and teacher, this long-established body is very active in geographical studies, and in electronic resources for them. The GA is dedicated to promoting the development of geography as a subject. It believes that geography makes both a distinctive and a wide contribution to education and that it is an essential component in preparing young people for life in the twenty-first century. The GA is also committed to providing support to all those who are engaged with it – whether out of personal interest or professionally. Click on the Resources link to see what they recommend

| | |
|---|---|
| Owner/Maintainer | Geographical Association, Sheffield, UK |
| Server location | Sheffield, UK |
| Authority | * * * * * |
| Ease of use | Good |
| Contact details given | Yes |
| Links | Good |
| Last update pre-visit | 20 |
| Alternative languages | No |
| Audience | Teachers. Students |
| Keywords | Teaching |

| | |
|---|---|
| Entry number | 46 |
| Title | *Royal Geographical Society (with the Institute of British Geographers) (RGS/IBG)* |
| URL | http://www.rgs.org/ |

Review

The RGS was formed in 1830, and thus has nearly two centuries of expertise in the field. Its early remit to support exploration now incorporates an ever-increasing emphasis on education, and the links reflect this in many ways. From an academic point of view, a good starting point to find out what it's all about, and to provide the big picture, especially within the UK. There is a full and varied lecture programme, with lectures taking place around the country, which is well worth keeping an eye on.

| | |
|---|---|
| Owner/Maintainer | Royal Geographical Society |
| Server location | London, UK |
| Authority | * * * * * the oldest in the UK |

| | |
|---|---|
| Ease of use | Very good – on pointing at each menu options there is a brief description of it |
| Contact details given | Postal address, telephone, fax and email |
| Links | Mostly internal, but externals at *Facts and Figures* page |
| Last update pre-visit | n.d. |
| Alternative languages | No |
| Audience | All with an interest in the subject |
| Keywords | Royal Geographical Society, Institute of British Geographers |

# Teaching

| | |
|---|---|
| Entry number | 47 |
| Title | *Computer Teaching Initiative (Geography, Geology and Meteorology)* |
| URL | http://www.geog.le.ac.uk/cti |

Review

Geography links from a group dedicated to the use of computing in education – this is the Geography, Geology and Meteorology group. *The Geo-Information Gateway* link leads to main menu headings Human g, Physical g, Geology, Environment, Cartography, Organisations etc. Selecting any of these leads to a sub-menu of web resources in the field, e.g. Human g. > Development g. > Centre for Development Studies (Copenhagen), which has its own links. Links to Geography in the News. Well laid out structure, information overload avoided.

| | |
|---|---|
| Owner/Maintainer | University of Leicester, UK |
| Server location | Leicester |
| Authority | * * * * Education quango |
| Ease of use | * * * * * |
| Contact details given | Yes |
| Links | Good, a few broken |
| Last update pre-visit | 531 |
| Alternative languages | No |

*General resources*

| Audience | Anyone with an interest, mainly academic |
| Keywords | Geology, Meteorology, News, Environment, Cartography, Development |

| Entry number | 48 |
| Title | *Geography Departments Worldwide* |
| URL | http://geowww.uibk.ac.at/geolinks/ |

Review

A searchable database of Geography Departments around the world. There are links to nearly 1,000 Departments in 85 Countries of which 765 have already signed the "Add Department Form" and thus can be searched by Country, Keyword and Research fields. Read the help page to make best use of the data. Very useful for finding who specialises in what where, for researchers.

| Owner/Maintainer | Klaus Foerster, Dept. of Geography, U. of Innsbruck |
| Server location | Innsbruck, Austria |
| Authority | * * * * * |
| Ease of use | Keyword search |
| Contact details given | Yes |
| Links | Only internal |
| Last update pre-visit | 24 days |
| Alternative languages | No |
| Audience | Academic |
| Keywords | Geography departments, Education |

| | |
|---|---|
| Entry number | 49 |
| Title | *Geography Discipline Network* |
| URL | http://www.chelt.ac.uk/gdn |

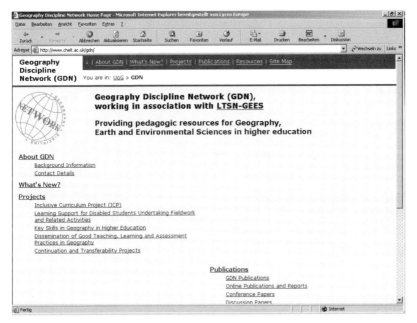

With kind permission of The Geography Discipline Network, University of Gloucestershire.

Review

This site provides pedagogic resources for Geography, Earth and Environmental Sciences in Higher Education. Home page includes What's New, GDN projects, Resource Database, Publications, Events, Archive and Links.

Click on Resource Database to get Case Studies of interesting teaching, learning and assessment practices in Geography, Earth and Environmental Sciences in Higher Education. Click on Links/Useful Geographic Resources to get around two dozen external links to good resources. Includes indexes and abstracts to *Journal of Geography in Higher Education, Journal of Geography* and *International Research in Geographical and Environmental Education.*

*General resources*

| | |
|---|---|
| Owner/Maintainer | Phil Gravestock, U. Gloucester |
| Server location | Cheltenham, UK |
| Authority | * * * * * |
| Ease of use | Clear navigation |
| Contact details given | Yes |
| Links | Alphabetical or by subject – well laid out |
| Last update pre-visit | 15 days |
| Alternative languages | No |
| Audience | Academic teachers and learning facilitators |
| Keywords | Teaching, Resources |

| | |
|---|---|
| Entry number | 50 |
| Title | *Virtual Geography Department Project (VGDP)* |
| URL | http://www.colorado.edu/geography/virtdept/contents.html |

Review

This project aims to interlink the curricula of geography departments both nationally and internationally using the Internet and World Wide Web. The goal of VGDP is to offer high quality curriculum materials and classroom and laboratory modules that can be used across the Internet by geography students and faculty at any university in the world, and to promote collaborative research. Stress is being placed on curriculum integration through the creation of on-line "electronic" texts and resource materials that will be of service to a wide range of departments. The project links existing materials already available on the Internet and, more importantly, has commissioned new materials to address topics not now represented on the Internet. In this way, geographers at many universities can share the time and expense of developing hypermedia and multimedia curriculum materials and benefit from the materials that might not otherwise be made available commercially. The Home page has direct links to Cartography,

Earths's Environment and Society, GIS/Remote Sensing/Statistics, History & Philosophy of Geography, Physicial g., Urban and Economian g., Virtual field trips, world, regional geography and area studies. Links to other such projects, e.g. Geography Discipline Network [entry 49].

| | |
|---|---|
| Owner/Maintainer | Anita Howard, U. of Colorado |
| Server location | U. of Colorado at Boulder, CO, USA |
| Authority | * * * * |
| Ease of use | Clear |
| Contact details given | Yes |
| Links | Good |
| Last update pre-visit | 170 |
| Alternative languages | No |
| Audience | Academic teachers and Learning Facilitators |
| Keywords | Teachers, Learning, Curriculum |

| | |
|---|---|
| Entry number | 51 |
| Title | *LTSN Subject Centre for Geography, Earth and Environmental Sciences (GEES)* |
| URL | http://www.gees.ac.uk |

Review

The Centre aims to become a major hub in the exchange of knowledge on learning and teaching across these subjects. Its principal aim is to encourage and disseminate good practice. Particular emphasis will be given to the ways of enhancing the quality of the students' learning experience, to include: promoting subject-based and key skills as the foundation for lifelong learning; encouraging the wider adoption of ICT, and providing guidance for the professional development of teaching and support staff. The services to be provided will include: Conferences; Departmental workshops; An individual enquiry / advisory service; Good practice databases; Electronic discussion lists; Registers of expertise; and Journals and Newsletters.

| | |
|---|---|
| Owner/Maintainer | Mick Sanders, U. of Plymouth, UK |
| Server location | Plymouth |
| Authority | * * * * |

*General resources*

| | |
|---|---|
| Ease of use | Clear |
| Contact details given | Yes |
| Links | Good |
| Last update pre-visit | n.d. |
| Alternative languages | No |
| Audience | Academic teachers and Learning Facilitators |
| Keywords | Earth Sciences, Environmental Sciences |

# Geography on the Web – By Category

## Area Studies

| | |
|---|---|
| Entry number | 52 |
| Title | *Aneki.com* |
| URL | http://www.aneki.com/lists |

Review

Aneki.com is an independent, privately operated website based in Montreal, Canada, dedicated to promoting wider knowledge of the world's countries and regions. It is a comprehensive source of continental and world rankings. Select region, then subject, to get the ranking, e.g. Wealth. The data for the compilations is derived from various sources, but principally the United States' Central Intelligence Agency's *World Factbook* [entry 53].

| | |
|---|---|
| Owner/Maintainer | Aneki.com |
| Server location | Montreal, Canada |
| Authority | * * * * * |
| Ease of use | Very simple |
| Contact details given | Yes |
| Links | Internal |
| Last update pre-visit | 39 days |
| Alternative languages | No |
| Audience | General |
| Keywords | Rankings, Statistics |

| Entry number | 53 |
|---|---|
| Title | *CIA World Factbook* |
| URL | http://www.odci.gov/cia/ publications/factbook/ |

Review
Annually updated collection of quick reference data on countries of the world, compiled by the USA's CIA (Central Intelligence Agency), and the basis for many statistical derivations. The main lists are Countries, Maps, Notes and Definitions, and Appendices.

The Countries list is very extensive, and clicking on the country of your choice brings up the flag and a map, with categories of Geography, People, Government, Economy, Communications, Transportation, Military, and Transnational Issues.

Comprehensive quick facts, but can be slow to load because of maps and graphics.

| Owner/Maintainer | CIA |
|---|---|
| Server location | Washington, DC, USA |
| Authority | * * * * * always check for date of data |
| Ease of use | * * * * * |
| Contact details given | Link to homepage |
| Links | Comprehensive internal database querying |
| Last update pre-visit | 63 days |
| Alternative languages | No |
| Audience | General. Business. Military |
| Keywords | Statistics, Maps |

| Entry number | 54 |
|---|---|
| Title | *Country-based search engines* |
| URL | http://www.philb.com/countryse.htm |

Review
This is simply a directory of search engines which are specific to 169 Continents, Countries and Regions (e.g. Baltic countries). Each country has a number indicating the number of search

engines relevant to it. Clicking on, for example, Fiji brings up three hyperlinks to follow. Or you can scroll through the list to see what's there, clicking as appropriate. Quickest way to get to Regional information.

| | |
|---|---|
| Owner/Maintainer | Phil Bradley |
| Server location | UK |
| Authority | * * * * * |
| Ease of use | Couldn't be simpler |
| Contact details given | Yes |
| Links | 1,540 |
| Last update pre-visit | 160 days |
| Alternative languages | No |
| Audience | General |
| Keywords | Countries, Regions, Areas |

| | |
|---|---|
| Entry number | 55 |
| Title | *Country Reports* |
| URL | http://www.countryreports.org/ |

Review

Formerly "A+ Country Reports", this is a commercial site owned by Emulate Me. In essence, a young person's version of the *CIA World Factbook* [entry 53], which gives basic profile statistics of countries in a clearly laid out format: Flag, history, maps, anthem, weather and current news. You can also get current weather conditions from a Home page link. A good, quick introduction to basic country data. An Advancer Profile is available on subscription.

| | |
|---|---|
| Owner/Maintainer | Emulate Me |
| Server location | USA |
| Authority | * * * * |
| Ease of use | * * * * * |
| Contact details given | Yes |
| Links | Internal |
| Last update pre-visit | n.d. |
| Alternative languages | No |
| Audience | General |
| Keywords | [All], Statistics |

*By Category*

Entry number       56
Title              *One World – Nations Online* (OWNO)
URL                http://www.nationsonline.org/
                   oneworld/

Review
At this site, you select from an index a country of interest, and
clicking on it brings up further links which originate in the
country concerned, e.g. for Malawi you get links to a political
map, Malawi news, a country guide, Official Statistics, Transportation, and a search option. Also sections on time, dates
and currencies.

Owner/Maintainer       Klaus Kästle
Server location        USA
Authority              * * * * Original sources
Ease of use            Good
Contact details given  Yes
Links                  Mainly unbroken
Last update pre-visit  2 days
Alternative languages  No
Audience               General. Academic
Keywords               Countries, Area Studies, Time,
                       Statistics, Cartography, News,
                       Transport


Entry number       57
Title              *IndiaStat*
URL                http://www.indiastat.com/

Review
This site provides an oceanic depth of India-specific, socio-
economic statistical facts and figures. Over half a million pages
of statistical data have been qualitatively analysed, condensed
and presented in a user-friendly format. This exhaustive and
methodically compiled data can easily be accessed within
three or four clicks. A useful feature is that all statistical information on the site can be converted into graphics using MS

Excel. Strongest in socio-economic data on various parameters including demographics, social welfare, electoral data, economy and the environment up to the district level. Includes World Population Clock and Did You Know ticker. To use this site you have to register as a member – annual fees are listed at /proceednavigt. asp?title=membership_fee

| | |
|---|---|
| Owner/Maintainer | Datanet India Pty Ltd. |
| Server location | New Delhi, India |
| Authority | * * * * * very comprehensive |
| Ease of use | Good |
| Contact details given | Yes |
| Links | Mainly internal |
| Last update pre-visit | n.d. |
| Alternative languages | No |
| Audience | General |
| Keywords | India, Population, Statistics, Demography, Welfare, Politics, Economy, Environment |

| | |
|---|---|
| Entry number | 58 |
| Title | *InfoNation* |
| URL | http://www.un.org/Pubs/ CyberSchoolBus/infonation/ info.asp |

Review

InfoNation is an easy-to-use, two-step database that allows you to view and compare the most up-to-date statistical data for the Member States of the United Nations. In the first menu, you can select up to five countries. Then you can proceed to the data menu where you will be able to select statistics and other data fields in up to four categories (Environment, Economy, Health, Technology), for instant comparison. Quick and neat.

| | |
|---|---|
| Owner/Maintainer | United Nations |
| Server location | NY, USA |
| Authority | * * * * * |

| | |
|---|---|
| Ease of use | Simple |
| Contact details given | Yes |
| Links | Internal |
| Last update pre-visit | n.d. |
| Alternative languages | Spanish, French |
| Audience | School. Academic. General |
| Keywords | Economy, Population, Social g |

| | |
|---|---|
| Entry number | 59 |
| Title | *ESDS International* |
| URL | http://www.esds.ac.uk/international/ |

Review

ESDS International provides access to, and support for, a range of international datasets – both macro and micro sources. The service aims to promote and facilitate increased and more effective use of international datasets in research, learning and teaching across a range of disciplines. There are web-based support materials including user guides, International data FAQs, case studies and exemplars. Access Data tells you what is available and how to get it. Follow the clear instructions and click through to the dataset of your choice.

| | |
|---|---|
| Owner/Maintainer | MIMAS (U. Manchester) and UK Data Archive (U. Essex) |
| Server location | Manchester, UK |
| Authority | * * * * * |
| Ease of use | Clear navigation |
| Contact details given | Yes |
| Links | Good |
| Last update pre-visit | 120 days |
| Alternative languages | Depends on language of dataset |
| Audience | Academic. General |
| Keywords | Area studies, statistics |

# Cartography

| | |
|---|---|
| Entry number | 60 |
| Title | *3G on W3: The Great Globe Gallery* |
| URL | http://main.amu.edu.pl/~zbzw/glob/ glob1.htm |

Review

This is a somewhat quirky site on the author's passion for the Earth as a sphere in space, Projections and Meteorology, but the maps and views are stunning in full colour. Most selections you make open in a separate window and, being graphics, are not speedy – but often worth the wait to re-consider our position in space and time.

| | |
|---|---|
| Owner/Maintainer | Zbigniew Zwolinski |
| Server location | Poland |
| Authority | * * * |
| Ease of use | Good |
| Contact details given | Yes |
| Links | 243 – some broken |
| Last update pre-visit | n.d. |
| Alternative languages | Polish (notes), some German |
| Audience | General |
| Keywords | Globes, Maps, Projections, Earth, Meteorology |

| | |
|---|---|
| Entry number | 61 |
| Title | *EDINA Digimap* |
| URL | http://edina.ac.uk/digimap |

Review

*Digimap* is an EDINA service that delivers Ordnance Survey Map Data to UK Tertiary Education. Data is available either to download to use with appropriate application software such as GIS or CAD, or as maps generated by *Digimap* online. *Digimap* allows users to view and print maps of any location in Great Britain at a series of predefined scales. Advanced tasks that *Digimap* enables are: downloading map data for use, for example, in GIS software on a user's own desktop; advanced cartographic tasks, such as user-specified scale, combining datasets on a map, large format printing and gazetteer functions on place names

| | |
|---|---|
| Owner/Maintainer | U. of Edinburgh |
| Server location | U. of Edinburgh, Scotland |
| Authority | * * * * * |
| Design | Clear |
| Ease-of-use | Subscription service – contact your Library for access details |
| Contact details given | Yes |
| Links | A few internal |
| Last update pre-visit | 480 days |
| Alternative languages | No |
| Audience | General |
| Keywords | Maps, Cartography, Ordnance Survey, GIS |

| | |
|---|---|
| Entry number | 62 |
| Title | *GEOnet Names Server (GNS)* |
| URL | http://gnswww.nima.mil/ geonames/gns/index.jsp |

Review

A database of non-US geographic names and features: over five million, updated monthly with names information approved by the US Board on Geographic Names.

Read the Help pages, then enter a place-name (free text), select a country from the drop-down list and it returns with designation (see help page), latitude and longitude.

Very useful for finding co-ordinates, for example to enter in software which calculates distances based on latitude and longitude, e.g. *How far from here to there?* [entry 63]

| | |
|---|---|
| Owner/Maintainer | US National Imagery and Mapping Agency |
| Server location | Bethesda, MD, USA |

| | |
|---|---|
| Authority | * * * * government agency, but some data rather old |
| Ease of use | Click and go |
| Contact details given | Yes |
| Links | Just internal database querying |
| Last update pre-visit | 6 days |
| Alternative languages | No |
| Audience | General |
| Keywords | Place-names, Latitude, Longitude, Co-ordinates |

| | |
|---|---|
| Entry number | 63 |
| Title | *How far from here to there?* |
| URL | http://www.obliquity.com/astro/distance.html |

Review

A handy little distance calculator, for which you need to know latitude and longitude – there is no look-up gazetteer, but you can use, for example, the GEOnet Names Server [entry 62].

| | |
|---|---|
| Owner/Maintainer | David Harper & Lynne Marie Stockman |
| Server location | USA |
| Authority | * * * * |
| Ease of use | Simple |
| Contact details given | Yes |
| Links | Not required |
| Last update pre-visit | 940 days |
| Alternative languages | None |
| Audience | General. Academic |
| Keywords | Latitude, Longitude |

*By Category*

| | |
|---|---|
| Entry number | 64 |
| Title | *International Boundaries Research Unit (IBRU)* |
| URL | http://www-ibru.dur.ac.uk/links |

Review

A unique resource of information and expertise on boundary and territorial issues. IBRU works to enhance the resources available for the peaceful resolution of such problems, including marine boundaries.

The Links page gives access to the specific issues. For the most recent information, see the Boundary and Security Bulletin link.

Simple instructions explain how to use the database effectively.

| | |
|---|---|
| Owner/Maintainer | International Boundaries Research Unit, University of Durham |
| Server location | University of Durham, UK |
| Authority | * * * * * this is the major source for boundary issues |
| Ease of use | Click and go |
| Contact details given | Yes |
| Links | Mainly database queries |
| Last update pre-visit | 208 days |
| Alternative languages | No |
| Audience | General |
| Keywords | Boundaries, Territorial disputes |

| | |
|---|---|
| Entry number | 65 |
| Title | *Ordnance Survey* |
| URL | http://www.ordsvy.gov.uk/ |

Review

The oldest mapping agency in the world, OS is a recognised market leader in its field. It offers a wider range of products than any comparable organisation, from traditional walking maps and road maps to the large-scale maps and digital products. Although OS is a UK government agency, it covers operating costs through sales of products, services and copyright licences. Click on the Education tab to see how OS contributes. Check the Terms and Conditions, and then select Get-a-map to print out a map of your choice centred on a place-name, postcode or grid reference (cf. http://www.streetmap.co.uk/) [entry 69A] There is a search facility to help you find what you want, plus a Glossary of Terms, and Geo Facts on the UK – how far is it REALLY from Land's End to John O'Groats?

| | |
|---|---|
| Owner/Maintainer | Ordnance Survey |
| Server location | Southampton, UK |
| Authority | * * * * *Original and best |
| Ease of use | Good |
| Contact details given | Yes |
| Links | Mainly internal |
| Last update pre-visit | n.d. |
| Alternative languages | Welsh |
| Audience | General |
| Keywords | Cartography, Maps |

| | |
|---|---|
| Entry number | 66 |
| Title | *Perry-Castaneda Library Map Collection (PCL)* |
| URL | http://www.lib.utexas.edu/maps/index.html |

Review

This is a large, well organised and easy to use collection of online map links. The first section is Online Maps of Special Interest (e.g. areas in the news), then Online Maps of General Interest, subdivided by World, Continents, and other regions (Middle East, Polar and Oceans, Russia and FSR, US, Texas, Texas Counties). Then follow links to Historical maps and Electronic cartographic resources. There is also a guide to the PCL Printed Map collection and an FAQ.

There many maps of many areas, selectable by date, scale and originating body. For example, there are detailed maps of

Johnston Atoll in the Pacific, and selecting Europe/Serbia and Montenegro/, gives seven General maps, four Detailed maps, eleven Regional and Former Yugoslavia maps and five Related maps. Links are also given to external sites with maps of the selected area.

| | |
|---|---|
| Owner/Maintainer | Perry-Castaneda Library |
| Server location | U. Texas, Austin, TX, USA |
| Authority | * * * * * |
| Ease-of-use | * * * * * |
| Contact details given | Yes |
| Links | well organised |
| Last update pre-visit | n.d. |
| Alternative languages | No |
| Audience | General |
| Keywords | Maps, Cartography |

| | |
|---|---|
| Entry number | 67 |
| Title | *Peters Projection Map* |
| URL | http://www.petersmap.com/table.html |

Review

First introduced by historian and cartographer Dr. Arno Peters in Germany in 1974, this new way of looking at the world generated stormy debate. The first English version of the map was published in 1983, and it continues to have passionate fans as well as staunch detractors. The earth is round. The challenge of any world map is to represent a round earth on a flat surface. There are literally thousands of map projections. Each has certain strengths and corresponding weaknesses. Choosing among them is an exercise in values clarification: you have to decide what's important to you. That is generally determined by the way you intend to use the map. The Peters Projection is an Area Accurate map, and challenges the mental Mercator that most of us carry round with us (see /page2.html for comparison).

| | |
|---|---|
| Owner/Maintainer | ODT, Inc. |
| Server location | Amherst, MA, USA |
| Authority | * * * * * |

| | |
|---|---|
| Ease of use | Good |
| Contact details given | Yes |
| Links | Internal |
| Last update pre-visit | n.d. |
| Alternative languages | No |
| Audience | General. Academic |
| Keywords | Cartography, Projections, Peters, Mercator |

| | |
|---|---|
| Entry number | 68 |
| Title | *Society of Cartographers* |
| URL | http://www.soc.org.uk/index.html |

Review

Founded in 1964, the Society's aims are to support the practising cartographer and encourage and maintain a high standard of cartographic illustration by providing information and opportunities to meet and exchange views and techniques with fellow practitioners cartographers, including relevant mapping software, downloadable by FTP.

| | |
|---|---|
| Owner/Maintainer | Society of Cartographers |
| Server location | U. Cambridge, UK |
| Authority | * * * * * Foremost mapping society in the UK |
| Ease of use | Good |
| Contact details given | Yes |
| Links | Good |
| Last update pre-visit | 5 days |
| Alternative languages | No |
| Audience | Academic, Cartographers, Mapmakers |
| Keywords | Maps, Cartography |

*By Category*

| | |
|---|---|
| Entry number | 69 [A & B] |
| Title | *Streetmap* [69A] |
| URL | http://www.streetmap.co.uk/ |

Review

This site provides address searching and street map facilities (with printout), for the UK, currently with street and road maps for the whole of mainland Britain. You can search by Street, London Street, Post Code, Latitude / Longitude, GB Place, OS grid reference, Telephone Code or Landranger grid to convert to other grids, and get a map. Indispensable for visiting unfamiliar Geography Departments, Libraries, Personnel Officers etc.

See also http://www.multimap.co.uk/ [69 B]

| | |
|---|---|
| Owner/Maintainer | Btex Ltd |
| Server location | UK |
| Authority | * * * * * Ordnance Survey and Bartholomew data |
| Ease of use | Select your grid start-point and then Search |
| Contact details given | Yes |
| Links | Internal |
| Last update pre-visit | n.d. |
| Alternative languages | No |
| Audience | General |
| Keywords | Place-names, Latitude, Longitude, Co-ordinates |

# CYBERGEOGRAPHY

| | |
|---|---|
| Entry number | 70 |
| Title | *Cyber Geography Research* |
| URL | http://www.cybergeography.org/ |

Review

A very new discipline within Geographical Studies, cybergeography is the study of the spatial nature of computer communications networks, particularly the Internet, the World-Wide

Web and other electronic "places" that exist behind our computer screens, popularly referred to as *cyberspace*. Cybergeography encompasses a wide range of geographical phenomena from the study of the physical infrastructure, traffic flows, the demographics of the new cyberspace communities, to the perception and visualisation of these new digital spaces. In addition, the potential geographical impacts of Cyberspace technologies on real-space needs to be examined. There are many geographies of cyberspace and many geographical approaches to study them. The emphasis of Cybergeography research tends to be on the more quantitative aspects of measuring and mapping the geography of cyberspaces. Clicking on Directory takes you to a somewhat eclectic list of information resources that help measure and map these new virtual geographies. Challenging and new.

| | |
|---|---|
| Owner/Maintainer | Martin Dodge, University College London |
| Server location | UCL, London, UK, with mirror sites round the world |
| Authority | * * * * * |
| Ease of use | Good |
| Contact details given | Yes |
| Links | Mainly internal |
| Last update pre-visit | 60 days |
| Alternative languages | No |
| Audience | Scientific. Academic |
| Keywords | Cybergeography |

# DEVELOPMENT

| | |
|---|---|
| Entry number | 71 |
| Title | *Human Development Reports (HDR)* |
| URL | http://hdr.undp.org |

Review
These reports are issued by the Human Development Reports Office, a part of the vast United Nations network, which produces authoritative reports on the development status of most nations with statistics and recommendations. Under Find Report, enter search term. The results are often downloadable in .pdf format. Special reports are also available by clicking on Other Publications and Papers on the home page and selecting Occasional Papers, which are often by subject rather than country, e.g. globalisation, transition economies. Invaluable.

| | |
|---|---|
| Owner/Maintainer | United Nations, New York |
| Server location | New York |
| Authority | * * * * *world body |
| Ease of use | Clear and navigable |
| Contact details given | Yes |
| Links | Mostly internal |
| Last update pre-visit | 8 days |
| Alternative languages | No |
| Audience | General. Academic |
| Keywords | Development, Statistics |

| | |
|---|---|
| Entry number | 72 |
| Title | *BLDS Bibliographic Databases* |
| URL | http://www.ids.ac.uk/blds/ |

Review
Web version of the British Library for Development Studies catalogue (BLDS), which is Europe's largest research collection on economic and social change in developing countries.

Click on Search the Catalogue, enter your search terms and view the results. There are also links to ejournals and on-line series.

Owner/Maintainer      Institute of Development Studies,
                      University of Sussex
Server location       University of Sussex, Brighton, UK
Authority             * * * * *
Ease of use           Click and go
Contact details given Yes
Links                 * * * * * very detailed
Last update pre-visit n.d.
Alternative languages Only for non-English databases
Audience              General. Academic
Keywords              Development, Human rights, Statistics


Entry number         73
Title                *ELDIS (Electronic Development and*
                     *Environment Information System)*
URL                  http://www.eldis.org

Review

ELDIS is a gateway to information sources on Development Studies and the Environment in the South, dealing principally with social, economic and political issues. Home page has a list of Guides, and the option to search free text (including using Boolean commands).

The Country Profiles option starts with broad continent-based groupings, and then selection of individual countries is possible from drop-down lists. Each country has sectoral pro-files (economics, education, environment), news, maps and statistics.

You can sign up for a monthly email update.

Owner/Maintainer      Institute of Development Studies,
                      University of Sussex, UK
Server location       University of Sussex, Brighton, UK
Authority             * * * * * materials are selected
Ease of use           * * * * *
Contact details given Yes
Links                 Good
Last update pre-visit 1 day

Alternative languages  No
Audience               General. Academic
Keywords               Social geography, Political geography,
                       Economic geography, Development,
                       Statistics, Environment, Maps, Statistics

# EARTH SCIENCES

Entry number          74
Title                 *USGS* (United States Geological
                      Survey)
URL                   http://www.usgs.gov/network/
                      index.html

With kind permission of the USGS.

Review
One of the major US government agencies, USGS provides links
to a wealth of information on many aspects of physical geography. From the main index page, you can select Information

on Biology, Earthquakes, Environment, EROS Data Center (EDC), Geology, Hazards, Maps, Marine Geology, Volcanoes and Water resources. The subsequent links aren't annotated, but are clear. Naturally, US-focussed.

| | |
|---|---|
| Owner/Maintainer | USGS |
| Server location | Reston, VA, USA |
| Authority | * * * * * |
| Ease of use | * * * * * |
| Contact details given | Yes |
| Links | Good |
| Last update pre-visit | 42 days |
| Alternative languages | No |
| Audience | General. Academic |
| Keywords | Biology, Earthquakes, Environment, Geology, Hazards, Maps, Marine Geology, Volcanoes, Water |

| | |
|---|---|
| Entry number | 75 |
| Title | *CSC Earth Science Server* |
| URL | http://www.csc.fi/earth_science/ earth_science.html |

Review

This site is designed to be easy to navigate, with a manageable number of links to relevant sites in the categories on the home page. A quick reference, Global Change Update is the first link, which include Geology, Geophysics, Environment and Remote Sensing, which further subdivide. Although the Geography sub-heading leads to only two links, one of those is the Yahoo Geography page, which has nineteen sub-categories and a page of general links.

A nice touch is the is the quotation at the top of each page.

| | |
|---|---|
| Owner/Maintainer | Ministry of Education, Finland |
| Location | Helsinki, Finland |
| Authority | * * * * * |
| Ease of use | Simple layered navigation |
| Contact details given | Yes |
| Links | Good quality |

*By Category*

| | |
|---|---|
| Last update pre-visit | 9 days |
| Alternative languages | Finnish |
| Audience | General. Academic |
| Keywords | Earth Sciences, Geology, Environment, Remote Sensing, Oceanography, Hydrology, Glaciology, Seismology, Geophysics |

| | |
|---|---|
| Entry number | 76 |
| Title | *Internet Resources in the Earth Sciences* |
| URL | http://www.lib.berkeley.edu/EART/ EarthLinks.html |

Review
Part of the University of California Library System, with good links once you get there. There are six major sub-divisions: Earth Sciences; Planetary Sciences; Geography; Geophysics/ Seismology; Climate and Weather; and Oceanography. Selecting Geography brings up Internet Resources in Maps and Cartography, which has a good (though subject undifferentiated) list with everything from a Balkan Atlas to Earthquake Hazard Maps for San Francisco.

| | |
|---|---|
| Owner/Maintainer | Library at the University of California, Berkeley, Los Angeles |
| Server location | University of California, Berkeley, Los Angeles, CA, USA |
| Authority | * * * * UCB has a strong Earth Sciences department |
| Ease of use | * * * * * |
| Contact details given | Yes |
| Links | Mostly American, but good quality |
| Last update pre-visit | 51 days |
| Alternative languages | No |
| Audience | Academic. Specialist |
| Keywords | Earth Sciences, Planetary Sciences, Geophysics, Seismology, Climatology, Oceanography |

# Environment

| | |
|---|---|
| Entry number | 77 |
| Title | *Natural Environment Research Council (NERC)* |
| URL | http://www.nerc.ac.uk/ |

Review

NERC is the British research council that does earth system science: advancing knowledge of planet Earth as a complex, interacting system. The work covers the full range of atmospheric, earth, terrestrial and aquatic sciences, from the depth of the oceans to the upper atmosphere. NERC provides independent research and training. The mission is to gather and apply knowledge, improve understanding and predict the behaviour of the natural environment and its resources. A full home page includes News, Funding details, Science Insight, Research centres and related websites.

| | |
|---|---|
| Owner/Maintainer | Natural Environment Research Council (NERC) |
| Server location | Swindon, UK |
| Authority | * * * * * |
| Ease of use | Good – home page provides plenty of options |
| Contact details given | Yes |
| Links | Good – internal and external |
| Last update pre-visit | 1 |
| Alternative languages | No |
| Audience | Environmentalists. Students. Teachers |
| Keywords | Atmospheric Sciences, Earth Observation, Geosciences, Hydrology, Marine Sciences, Polar Sciences, Environment |

# Geographic Information Systems

| | |
|---|---|
| Entry number | 78 |
| Title | *GIS Dictionary* |
| URL | http://www.geo.ed.ac.uk/ agidict/welcome.html |

Review
This is a dictionary of Geographic Information Systems terminology, searchable in free text alphabetically, by category (e.g. Cartography, Photogrammetry) or by acronym. If you want to know what kriging is, or what a MEGRIN is, this is the place to look. Results screen has further references. A useful source for GIS students, still being enlarged.

| | |
|---|---|
| Owner/Maintainer | Association for Geographic Information and Dept. of Geography, Edinburgh U. |
| Server location | U. Edinburgh, Scotland |
| Authority | * * * * * |
| Ease of use | Very simple |
| Contact details given | Yes |
| Links | Internal |
| Last update pre-visit | n.d. |
| Alternative languages | No |
| Audience | General. Academic |
| Keywords | GIS, Remote Sensing, Photogrammetry, Dictionaries |

# Meteorology

| | |
|---|---|
| Entry number | 79 |
| Title | *World Meteorological Organization (WMO)* |
| URL | http://www.wmo.ch/index-en.html |

Review

Founded in 1951, the WMO is a specialised agency of the United Nations, co-ordinating global scientific activity to allow increasingly prompt and accurate weather information for public, private and commercial use.

The Index page has a useful About Us summary and a search facility. There are also direct links to Major Issues, Hot Topics and Library. There is also the option to search by WMO Programme or from an alphabetical topic list. Uses a ticker for further explanation. Uses scrollable frames, easy to navigate.

At the page /web-en/member.html is a list of the 185 members, so you can go directly to meteorological information on any country of interest.

| | |
|---|---|
| Owner/Maintainer | WMO |
| Server location | Geneva, Switzerland |
| Authority | * * * * * |
| Ease of use | Click and go |
| Contact details given | Yes |
| Links | Very good – especially for access to member countries |
| Last update pre-visit | 1 day |
| Alternative languages | French, Spanish |
| Audience | General |
| Keywords | Meteorology, Weather, Climate, Atmosphere |

| | |
|---|---|
| Entry number | 80 |
| Title | *Meteorological Office, UK* |
| URL | http://www.meto.gov.uk/ |

Review

One of the world's leading meteorology centres. A variety of services meet a wide range of interests, from the general public, government and schools, through broadcasters and online media, to civil aviation and almost every other industry sector in the UK and around the world. There is a huge amount of public access weather data and forecasts, including UK, world and city forecasts, weather warnings, UV index, charts, marine information and satellite imagery. Also a useful FAQ for queries such as F/C conversions. There are links to national meteorological organisations, related scientific sites (including satellite data) and sites using their data.

| | |
|---|---|
| Owner/Maintainer | Meteorological Office, UK |
| Server location | Bracknell/Exeter, UK |
| Authority | * * * * * top site |
| Ease of use | * * * * * |
| Contact details given | Yes |
| Links | * * * * * many and varied |
| Last update pre-visit | 1 day |
| Alternative languages | No |
| Audience | General. Academic |
| Keywords | Atmosphere, Weather, Climate, Meteorology |

# Oceanography

| | |
|---|---|
| Entry number | 81 |
| Title | *National Oceanographic and Atmospheric Administration (NOAA)* |
| URL | http://www.noaa.gov/ |

Review

Founded in 1970, NOAA is one of the world's leading government scientific organisations for monitoring and research in atmosphere, weather, climate, meteorology and oceanography.

The homepage offers many internal and external links, including the above subjects plus fisheries and satellites, News (headlines and in-depth). You can search the Library catalogue.

| | |
|---|---|
| Owner/Maintainer | NOAA (U.S. Government) |
| Server location | Washington, DC, USA |
| Authority | * * * * * |
| Ease of use | Click and go |
| Contact details given | Yes |
| Links | Mainly internal (government organisations), but many external |
| Last update pre-visit | 1 day |
| Alternative languages | No |
| Audience | General. Scientific. Academic |
| Keywords | Oceanography, Atmosphere, Weather, Climate, Meteorology |

| | |
|---|---|
| Entry number | 82 |
| Title | *Ocean Biogeographic Information System (OBIS)* |
| URL | http://www.iobis.org/ |

Review

Part of the Centre of Marine Life Program, OBIS is a web-based provider of global geo-referenced information on accurately identified marine species. It contains expert species level and habitat level databases and provides a variety of spatial query tools for visualising relationships among species and their environment. OBIS strives to assess and integrate biological, physical, and chemical oceanographic data from multiple sources. Users of OBIS, including researchers, students, and environmental managers, gain a dynamic view of the multi-dimensional oceanic world. Includes useful lesson plans. The home page contains links to many resources, particularly in education and technology.

| | |
|---|---|
| Owner/Maintainer | Rutgers University |
| Server location | Rutgers U., NJ, USA |
| Authority | * * * * Original sources |
| Ease of use | Good |
| Contact details given | Yes |
| Links | Good – very international |
| Last update pre-visit | 14 days |
| Alternative languages | No |
| Audience | General. Academic |
| Keywords | Marine Studies, Marine species, Oceanography |

| | |
|---|---|
| Entry number | 83 |
| Title | *Scripps Institution of Oceanography (SIO)* |
| URL | http://sio.ucsd.edu/ |

Review

Founded in 1903, SIO is involved in global oceanographic science research. Research programmes include physical, chemical, biological, geological and geophysical studies of the oceans.

The homepage has buttons for news, research, education and resources.

The last includes Scripps Library, which is very useful, linking directly to MELVYL, the University of California's library catalogues and databases, and Internet Guides and databases to locate resources.

| | |
|---|---|
| Owner/Maintainer | SIO |
| Server location | University of California, San Diego, CA, USA |

| | |
|---|---|
| Authority | * * * * * |
| Ease of use | * * * * * |
| Contact details given | Yes |
| Links | * * * * * |
| Last update pre-visit | 164 days |
| Alternative languages | No |
| Audience | General. Academic |
| Keywords | Oceanography, Atmosphere, Weather, Climate, Meteorology, Earthquakes, Erosion |

| | |
|---|---|
| Entry number | 84 |
| Title | *Woods Hole Oceanographic Institution (WHOI)* |
| URL | http://www.whoi.edu/ |

Review

Founded in 1930, Woods Hole is a world leader in oceano-graphic research. The Internet service has been running since 1994, and the homepage is full of options, divided into Welcome and At Sea. There are free text searching options, and there is also a direct link to the MBL/WHOI Library.

| | |
|---|---|
| Owner/Maintainer | Woods Hole Oceanographic Institution |
| Server location | Woods Hole, MN, USA |
| Authority | * * * * * Long established |
| Ease of use | Click and go |
| Contact details given | Yes |
| Links | * * * * * |
| Last update pre-visit | n.d. |
| Alternative languages | No |
| Audience | Specialist. Academic |
| Keywords | Oceanography, Geology |

# Population

| | |
|---|---|
| Entry number | 85 |
| Title | *International Database* [of Census information] (IDB) |
| URL | http://www.census.gov/ipc/www/idbnew.html |

Review

The IDB combines data from country sources (especially censuses and surveys) with The International Population Centre's (IPC) estimates and projections to provide information dating back as far as 1950 and as far ahead as 2050. The major types of data available in the IDB include: Population by age and sex, Vital rates, Infant mortality and life tables, Fertility and child survivorship, Migration, Marital Status, Family planning, Ethnicity, religion, and language, Literacy, Labour force, Employment, and Income and Households. Data characteristics include: Temporal: Selected years, 1950-present, projected demographic data to 2050. Spatial: 227 countries and areas. Resolution: National population, selected data by urban/rural residence, selected data by age and sex. The Dynamic tool is a very appealing way of viewing changing data over times! Sources of the data include: U.S. Bureau of the Census, Estimates and Projections, National Statistics Offices, United Nations and Specialized Agencies (ILO, UNESCO, WHO).

| | |
|---|---|
| Owner/Maintainer | US Census Bureau |
| Server location | Washington, DC, USA |
| Authority | * * * * * |
| Ease of use | Good – follow the prompts to construct your query |
| Contact details given | Yes |
| Links | Mainly internal |
| Last update pre-visit | 36 days |
| Alternative languages | No |
| Audience | General |
| Keywords | Population, Statistics, Demography, Countries, Area Studies |

Entry number        86
Title        *Population Index*
URL        http://popindex.princeton.edu/

Review

A major source of population data. This bibliography is designed to cover the world's demographic and population literature, including books and other monographs, serial publications, journal articles, working papers, doctoral dissertations, and machine-readable data files. It provides a search interface to the entire *Population Index* database for 1986-2000, a total of 46,035 citations. You can search the database by author, subject, region or free-text appearing anywhere in a citation. Queries may be restricted by giving a year or range of years. Also includes annual cumulative indexes for authors and geographic regions. The *User's Guide* is an excellent introduction to getting the most of the database. For example, if you are studying the migration of women in Latin America, type this into the relevant boxes at the Search screen, and you will get (about) 16 hits. By using the Browse button, and then Cumulative indices, select the authors' names to see the full abstract, and consequently whether the articles are of use to you.

| | |
|---|---|
| Owner/Maintainer | Princeton University |
| Server location | Princeton, NJ, USA |
| Authority | * * * * * |
| Ease of use | Good |
| Contact details given | Yes |
| Links | Internal, to the abstracts |
| Last update pre-visit | n.d. |
| Alternative languages | Where relevant (i.e. source document) |
| Audience | Academic, General |
| Keywords | Population; Demography |

# Remote Sensing

| | |
|---|---|
| Entry number | 87 |
| Title | *SIR-C/X-SAR Images* |
| URL | http://www.jpl.nasa.gov/radar/ sircxsar |

Review

This tongue-twistingly named site is a joint US-German-Italian project which uses imaging radar to capture images of the earth that are useful in many disciplines. Categories covered are Archaeology, Cities, Interferometry, Snow, Ice and Glaciers, Ecology and Agriculture, Geology, Oceans, Rivers, Volcanoes.

Selecting an image brings up a brief geographical description of the area, the techniques used by the imaging system in capturing the data, and options for different resolutions with which to view the image. Current information is available from the NASA/IPL Imaging Radar Program link.

| | |
|---|---|
| Owner/Maintainer | Jet Propulsion Laboratory, NASA |
| Server location | Jet Propulsion Laboratory, Pasadena, CA, USA |
| Authority | * * * * * long established government laboratory |
| Ease of use | Click and go |
| Contact details given | Yes |
| Links | Mostly internal – database querying |
| Last update pre-visit | n.d. |
| Alternative languages | No |
| Audience | General |
| Keywords | Remote sensing, Urban geography, Ecology, Geology, Oceans, Rivers, Volcanoes |

# Tourism

| | |
|---|---|
| Entry number | 88 |
| Title | *Geography of Leisure and Tourism Research Group (GLTRG)* |
| URL | http://www.ex.ac.uk/geography/tourism/gltrg/welcome.html |

Review

GLTRG is a new Research Group of the RGS/IBG [entry 46]. It aims to advance and promote geographical research and knowledge into leisure and tourism. It publishes a Newsletter, list of events, and has good links to other research study groups in this field.

| | |
|---|---|
| Owner/Maintainer | Tim Coles, Dept. of Geography, U. of Exeter |
| Server location | Exeter, UK |
| Authority | * * * * Respected organisation |
| Ease of use | Click and go |
| Contact details given | Yes |
| Links | Mostly internal |
| Last update pre-visit | 1000 days |
| Alternative languages | No |
| Audience | Academic, Researchers |
| Keywords | Tourism |

# Urban Studies

| | |
|---|---|
| Entry number | 89 |
| Title | *Resource for Urban Design Information (RUDI)* |
| URL | http://www.rudi.net/news.cfm |

Review

RUDI is a multimedia Internet resource for teaching, research and professional activity in urban design and its related disciplines. Urban design in this context includes the physical

design, management, planning and use of buildings and land-
scape in terms of their relationship to public and open space.
On the home page there are news and latest resources links,
and frame links to a search option and an A-Z site index.
Bookshelf contains bibliographies and new works, both printed
and online, in the field. What's on RUDI is a virtual library
containing both full-text documents and excerpts. You need to
log in to get the full benefits.

| | |
|---|---|
| Owner/Maintainer | Oxford Brookes University |
| Server location | Oxford, UK |
| Authority | * * * * * |
| Ease of use | Good |
| Contact details given | Yes |
| Links | Internal |
| Last update pre-visit | n.d. |
| Alternative languages | No |
| Audience | General |
| Keywords | Urban g., Design, Environment, Town Planning |

# Indexes

## Site name

*Indexes*

*Indexes*

# URL

*Indexes*

*Indexes*

# Keyword

| Keyword* | Entry |
|---|---|
| Agriculture | 14, 59, 72, 87 |
| Archaeology | 87 |
| Astronomy | 39, 60, 76 |
| Atlases see Cartography | |
| Atmosphere *see* Meteorology | |
| Boundaries | 64 |
| Cartography | 9, 10, 12, 14, 15, 17, 22, 24, 25, 26, 27, 34, 39, 47, 52, 53, 54, 56, 60, 61, 62, 64, 65, 66, 67, 68, 69A, 69B, 73, 74, 88 |
| Census *see* Population | |
| Climatology *see* Meteorology | |
| Cybergeography | 70 |
| Data *see* Statistics | |
| Demography see Population | |
| Development | 13, 40, 47, 59, 71, 72, 73 |
| Earth sciences | 17, 38, 49, 51, 74, 75, 76, 77, 83 |
| Earthquakes *see* Seismology | |
| Ecology | 38, 87 |
| Economics | 9, 27, 42, 50, 52, 53, 54, 57, 58, 59, 72, 73 |
| Energy | 14, 59 |
| Environment | 13, 15, 18, 19, 38, 39, 40, 47, 49, 50, 51, 53, 57, 59, 72, 73, 74, 75 77 89 |
| Erosion | 83 |
| Fisheries | 81 |
| Flags | 24, 52, 54 |
| Geochemistry | 17, 84 |

---

* *NB* Many sites in the General Resources entries can be searched using any keyword – this is a list of non-hierarchichal terms principally for the Subject Categories.

103

*Indexes*

# Guides to Information Sources

### Information Sources in Music

Edited by Lewis Foreman
2003. xix, 445 pages. Hardbound. € 110.00
ISBN 3-598-24441-X

From medieval chorales, to light operetta, to electronically generated 'musique concrete', this title offers meticulous coverage of musical composition and criticism, past and present.

**Information Sources in Music** is an easy-to-use, evaluative guide to the wide range of published sources of information available. Arranged by subject, each entry includes a brief description of the source, frequency of publication, and price and serial information where appropriate. As a time-saving resource this title will enable researchers to go straight to the information they need, indicating the range of sources available and offering a means of assessing which are the most useful.

---

### Information Sources in the Social Sciences

Edited by David Fisher, Terry Hanstock and Sandra Price
2002. xv, 511 pages. Hardbound. € 110.00
ISBN 3-598-24439-8

This title is an evaluative Guide to the sources of information in the social sciences. It provides guidance on the key sources in each of the areas that make up the social sciences.

This title in the information sources series will appeal to those studying and teaching social sciences and its competent subjects. Contents include: A general guide to the literature of the Social Sciences, General Social Science Information Sources, Anthropology, Economics, Education, Human Services, Law/Criminology, Political Science; Psychology; Public administration, Bibliographies and much more besides.

**K·G·Saur Verlag**
A Thomson Learning Company
Postfach 70 16 20 · D-81316 München · Germany · Tel. +49 (0)89 7 69 02-232
Fax +49 (0)89 7 69 02-250 · e-mail: info@saur.de · http://www.saur.de

# Resource Guides to

## Online Business Sourcebook 2003
Including Online, CD-ROM and Web Products

Edited by Pamela Foster
2003. X, 402 pages. Hardbound € 298.00 / sFr 513.00
ISBN 3-598-11528-8

*Online Business Sourcebook* is a unique evaluative guide to electronic business database products and services. It is designed to indicate to the business user those products that are likely to be of most use in searching for a particular category of information.

The sourcebook is unique in several ways:
• It deals with the full range of business database products and services in a single volume
• It evaluates many products, rather than merely describing them
• It is selective, presenting information on the most important products
• It includes online, Web, CD-ROM and diskettes products
• For most companies and organizations, it contains full contact details
• Incorporated are three indexes (name, country/regions and subject)

The editor, Pam Foster, brings many years of experience to the sourcebook. She has personally tested many of the products featured so the user benefits from her expertise.


## Ethical and Socially Responsible Investment
A Reference Guide for Researchers

By Dominic Broadhurst, Janette Watson and Jane Marshall
Introduction by Petra Molthan
2003. XXV, 178 pages. Hardbound. € 98.00 / sFr 169.00
IBSN 3-598-24630-7

*Ethical and Socially Responsible Investment* is a growing area of interest with an ever greater array of investment funds and financial products in this area on offer to private individuals. Moreover individuals and government bodies are also more aware of these issues and their impact, hence their need to become informed of the source materials in this book. Companies are also now more accountable to their customers and shareholders in these areas, and this continues to increase.

# Business Information Sources

This book is the first major authoritative guide to enable researchers and readers to have the sources they need close to hand.

This book provides its readers with an extensive guide to sources. The guide is comprehensive and organised in a userfriendly way, looking at the main topics of interest and relevance. Each entry is evaluated and full contact details are provided.

Dominic Broadhurst, Jane Marshall and Janette Watson are all staff of the Manchester Business School. They have extensive experience of providing SRI research services and have selected the entries based on their usefulness and relevance.

In her informative introduction, Petra Molthan includes the history and principles of SRI, giving readers a useful background to the subject.

## Business Information Handbook 2003

Edited by David Mort
2003. VIII, 218 pages. Hardbound. € 128.00 / sFr 220.00
ISBN 3-598-11501-6

The *Business Information Handbook 2003* is a new sourcebook which not only describes the major sources of business information but also considers the role of business information in the business process and considers the recent changes brought about in sources and delivery by the new Web-based technologies. In addition, there are case studies from business information specialists which provide practical insights into the use of busi-ness information.

The guide not only provides an introduction to business information but it also acts as an update for more experienced information specialists and researchers working in the increas-ingly changing world of business information.

The book is edited by David Mort, Director, IRN Research and David has also compiled most of the chapters. David has worked at a senior level in the UK business information sector for 20 years. Other experienced information professionals and researchers contributing including Gary Giddings and Sophie Gerrard, also from IRN Research, and Margaret Brittin, founder and co-partner in information consultancy Information Unlimited. Case study contributors include Stella Trench (AIG), Jan Whittington (Advent International), Catherine Cosgrove (Institute of Petroleum), Jim Tudor (Bournemouth University).

**K·G·Saur Verlag**
A Thomson Learning Company
Postfach 70 16 20 · D-81316 München · Germany · Tel. +49 (0)89 769 02-232
Fax +49 (0)89 769 02-250 · e-mail: info@saur.de · http://www.saur.de